Tips for Reading Together

Children learn best when reading is fun.

- Talk about the title and the picture on the front cover.
- Look through the pictures so your child can see what the story is about.
- Read the story to your child, placing your finger under each word as you read.
- Read the story again and encourage your child to join in.
- Give lots of praise as your child reads with you.

Children enjoy re-reading stories and this helps to build their confidence.

Have fun!

After you have read the story, find the feather hidden in every picture.

This book includes these useful common words:
the get my said

For more hints and tips on helping your child become a successful and enthusiastic reader look at our website www.oxfordowl.co.uk.

Mum's New Hat

Written by Roderick Hunt
Illustrated by Alex Brychta

OXFORD
UNIVERSITY PRESS

4

Mum had a new hat.

The wind blew.

It blew Mum's hat off.

"Get my hat," said Mum.

Dad ran.

The wind blew.

Oh no!

"Get that hat," said Dad.

Kipper ran.

The wind blew.

Oh no!

"Get that hat," said Kipper.

Biff ran.

The wind blew.

Oh no!

"Look at my new hat!"
said Mum.

Talk about the story

How did Mum lose her new hat?

Why do you think Biff has a camera?

What funny things happened to Mum's hat?

What has happened to you on windy days?

A maze

Help Mum get her hat.

Read with Biff, Chip and Kipper offers two important pathways to learning to read. **First Stories** have been specially written to provide practice in reading everyday language, and the **Phonics** stories help children practise reading by decoding sounds in words, as they learn to do in school.

Books at Level 2: Starting to read

Look out for the next level: Becoming a reader

UNIVERSITY PRESS

Great Clarendon Street, Oxford OX2 6DP
Text © Roderick Hunt 2006
Illustrations © Alex Brychta 2006
First published 2006. This edition published 2014
Series Editors: Kate Ruttle, Annemarie Young

British Library Cataloguing in Publication
Data available
ISBN: 978-0-19-273985-8
10 9 8 7 6 5 4 3 2 1
Printed in China by Imago
The characters in this work are the original creation of
Roderick Hunt and Alex Brychta who retain copyright
in the characters.